To
you.

Library of Congress
Cataloging-in-Publication Data

Hanson, Warren.
  What Really Matters / written and illustrated by Warren Hanson.
    p. cm.
  ISBN 978-0-931674-78-5 (alk. paper)
  1. Love. 2. Values. I. Title.
  BF575.L8H336 2012
  177'.7--dc23

                                    2012007870

TRISTAN PUBLISHING, INC.
2355 Louisiana Avenue North
Golden Valley, MN 55427

Please visit us at:
www.tristanpublishing.com
books with a message

Life is complicated.

It grows more so every day.
But if I know what really matters,
I will never lose my way.

But...

how do I know what really matters?
And how will I recognize
what should really be important?

What will it take to make me wise?

It can seem that what's important
is what other people see.
What matters more? What I believe in?
Or what others think of me?

I am sure my *family* matters.

We're entwined with one another —
husband, wife, daughter, son,
mother, father, sister, brother.

We have shared the worst and best of life
together through the years.
All the happiness and heartache,
all the laughter and the tears.

I am grateful for *good health,*

but would it matter to me more
if tomorrow, suddenly,

I didn't have it anymore?

Does the country that I come from,

or the color of my skin,

or the language that I speak

say who I really am within?

And what about my *faith*?

Does it really guide my way?

Does belief in something bigger
make me better every day?

Does *money* really matter?

It can do a lot of good,

but does it matter more if I have less
than what I think I should?

Is *yesterday* important?

Can mistakes of long ago
be corrected, so the life I have today is perfect?

No.

And what about *tomorrow*?

Don't I worry and I fret
about the bad things that could happen
that just haven't happened yet?

And yet, the past has made me who I am.

And I've turned out okay.

While the future holds the goals
that I am working toward today.

And my *career*?

My *friends*?

My *hobbies*?

They are all important, too.

But I have only so much *time*,

and so it matters what I do.

And in that time that I've been given,
there's one thing I need to see...

makes all things matter.

And that love
begins with me.

If I have  *Love*,

then I can bear all things,
can pass the toughest test.

If I have *Love*,

I can believe all things
will turn out for the best.

If I have *Love*,

I have the hope that
all the world can work for good.

If I have *Love*,

I can endure what, without love,
I never could.

Love goes on forever,

farther than the heart can see.

Love

makes all things matter.

And the rest
is up to me.

I must decide whether it matters
how much money I can make.

Or where I live. Or what I drive.
Or what vacations I can take.

Or if it matters that my skin
is brown or white or tan.

How or where I talk to God.
If I'm a woman or a man.

If I'm left or if I'm right
or if I'm smart or if I'm not.

The diplomas I've collected.
Or the trophies that I've got.

These decisions have a purpose.
They provide a place to start
to make a life that really matters,

starting here,

in my own heart.

If I have  Love,

all things can work for good.
I only have to look.

What really matters
is what I will do...

after I close this book.